GET IT DONE

The Journey to Entrepreneurship
From Idea to Open

Dr. Rose Emily Lorenzo

Best of luck
Dr. Rose

The resources in this book are provided for informational purposes only and should not be used to replace the specialized training and professional judgment of a health care or mental health care professional.

Neither the author nor the publisher can be held responsible for the use of the information provided within this book. Please always consult a trained professional before making any decision regarding treatment of yourself or others.

ISBN: 9780578715759
EPUB: 9780578715766

Edited by Adriana Perez
Cover design by 100 Covers
Formatted by Robin L Reed

READ FIRST:

Download the Get It Done Workbook **Free**

I found that readers have the most success with my book when they use the Get It Done Workbook as they read.

Just to say thanks for downloading my book, I'd like to give you the Get It Done Workbook 100% Free.

CLICK HERE TO DOWNLOAD

www.drroselorenzo.com

DEDICATION

I am so grateful every day for the ability to learn and teach others. I thank God for His unwavering love and support through this process. This book is dedicated to all family, friends, colleagues, and entrepreneurs who have supported and encouraged me each step of this journey and in my life. My life continues to be an incredible journey because of all the people I am fortunate enough to know. I know that God is good every day, and every day God is good!

"Build your own dreams, or someone else will hire you to build theirs."

— Farrah Gray

Contents

Foreword

I made many of the most basic mistakes that small business owners often make during my own journey to entrepreneurship, having owned and operated several small businesses ranging from a film production company to commercial cleaning. However, from those mistakes came significant learning experiences that allowed me to share with other small business owners who were experiencing the same or similar business errors. During my reflection of the entrepreneurial journey, I discovered there was so much information that I did not know when I first started my business. And what's more, most of what I did know was lousy information or not relevant to my business.

Throughout my travels, I have come across many people who have incredible ideas and the desire to own a business but find themselves asking, where do I begin? I have always been fascinated by stories of people who state they started a business with little to no money, and now their business is a global enterprise. How did they do that? What were the skills necessary to achieve such success? Did they have a mentor or someone who showed them the ropes?

If you ever thought you wanted to start a business and were unsure of where to start, this book will provide you with information on how to start and sustain a business. Beginning with the entrepreneur mindset, this book will guide you through topics like creating your business from an idea or concept, developing a mission and vision statement, knowing your customer, the importance of a business plan, business formations, branding, understanding finances, taxes, and human capital. Ultimately, it can help you develop a clear picture of your business and the direction you need to go to get started.

I would like to share the information that no one shared with me when I first decided to become an entrepreneur. The decision to become an entrepreneur was about freedom, flexibility, and the ability to help people anywhere, not solely in the city where I lived. This book will provide you with the tools necessary to create an excellent plan for your new or existing business.

CHAPTER ONE

Start Your Journey

So, you want to become an entrepreneur. Congratulations! Becoming an entrepreneur is an exciting moment in a person's life. It is making the decision to follow one's dream and accomplish a self-made success. Humans, by nature, are innovators and entrepreneurs. We yearn to discover our world and push incredible boundaries to do so. We thirst for adventure, freedom, knowledge, and opportunity. Having your own business offers freedom from authority, the ability to pursue your passions, infinite financial prospects, and plenty of excitement. With today's technologies and global market opportunities, the sky is limitless. The thrill of being your own boss is really the independence of having your own business. Growing it is based on the amount of effort that you put into your business. Being the boss is fun and exciting. It is enjoyable to be able to get up and to plan each day. While that joy comes with upsides and downsides, I enjoy running my own business and having the opportunity to carry out ideas.

WHAT IS AN ENTREPRENEUR?

Entrepreneurs are characterized as business owners, innovators, and even political or religious leaders. Entrepreneurship is the basis of the economic climate and framework of American culture. Entrepreneurs are individuals who embody the tenacity to create and achieve a vision.

According to the U.S. Small Business Administration (SBA), the turnover rate of small businesses at the end of 2017 was substantial. The SBA noted that in 2018, entrepreneurs established 414,000 start-up businesses. In the same year, 396,000 (87%) of the companies discontinued operations, causing a loss of approximately 792,000 jobs.

Entrepreneurs employ 59 million individuals, amounting to 48% of the private workforce. Unfortunately, according to the American FactFinder, the percent of business failure each year is 22% for exclusively female-owned businesses and 3% for solely male-owned companies.

The lack of entrepreneurial knowledge is a significant contributor to otherwise preventable business failure. Knowledge is highly dependable on research and information literacy skills and knowing when information is needed.

Understanding how to acquire knowledge and access information includes awareness of various forms of assistance and informational resources, as well as the ability to utilize resources such as utilizing Small Business Development Centers, libraries, and the Internet.

The Bureau of Labor Statistics stated in 2019 that 68.7% of businesses with employees are still in operations by the second year of business establishment. Half of those businesses are still operating by the fifth year of business inception. Of the small businesses which are still operational after the second year of start-up, one-third of the companies succeed in the first year.

Many entrepreneurs often have a difficult time maintaining their initial vision and decide to shut down operations, which could be associated with the number of businesses that close by the second year of operations. Becoming an entrepreneur means developing a specific mindset, known as the entrepreneurial mindset.

ENTREPRENEURIAL MINDSET

Entrepreneurs are creative, innovative, and resilient. The first step to entrepreneurship is developing an entrepreneurial mindset. What does it mean to develop an entrepreneurial mindset? It means embodying a way of thinking that enables you to overcome challenges, be decisive, and accept responsibility for your outcomes. It is a constant need to improve your skills, learn from your mistakes, and take continuous action on your ideas. It is recognizing that your idea will serve the community or society as a service or product.

From my experience, everyone has a great idea that could create a successful business. However, not everyone has the tenacity or the mindset to become an entrepreneur.

Why, you ask? Primarily because becoming an entrepreneur involves accepting a certain level of risk, a lack of job security with benefits, a lack of a consistent salary, and more than a forty-hour workweek.

From the onset, becoming an entrepreneur requires a lot of research regarding:

- the type of business formation needed

- identifying how to register your business

- which accounting software to use

- how to market the product or service

One must also determine the need for a social media or eCommerce site. Branding your business requires establishing a logo, website, mission, and vision before one can decide how that brand will be introduced to the public.

Questions to ask yourself are:

Do I have the mindset to become an entrepreneur? How can I take a great product or service from concept to market? Do I have the personality to be the boss? Am I willing to risk time and money to make my dream a reality? Can I handle the physical and emotional strain of hard work and uncertainty?

It helps to look at others who have succeeded. As you will discover, success doesn't come easy. It takes a plan, the right skills, and lots of determination. Mistakes and bad luck are part of the game. Still, tenacity and mindset, driven by a specific goal, along with some elbow grease, can turn a unique idea into a reality—one in which you are the boss.

Before working as a business consultant for the past three decades, I owned and operated several businesses. I always had the intention of great success with each endeavor. However, operating with the wrong information that I received either from friends, other business owners, or the Internet, I made more mistakes than I care to admit.

And yet, those mistakes taught me how to become a successful entrepreneur. Through my education and research, the lessons learned have allowed me to help many small business owners in business growth and sustainability.

I would like to share the information gained through this journey that no one shared with me when I first decided to become an entrepreneur.

I wasn't always an entrepreneur, but I felt like I had the mindset to become one. I had many years in banking, finance, and accounting; jobs that I liked but did not love. The corporate politics were often more than I wanted to deal with daily.

I decided to live by my motto, *"if you are not happy going where you are going, go somewhere else."* So, I decided to leave the stability of the corporate environment and emerge as an entrepreneur.

The first business I started was a t-shirt apparel company. What? I knew nothing about the apparel business, but the idea was great: to create t-shirts of the legendary African American artists. The research showed that there were no t-shirts with artists like Dorothy Dandridge, Lena Horne, Duke Ellington,

Miles Davis, etc. These were artists that paved the way in the entertainment industry.

There was a market for these shirts, but the problem was I still didn't have experience in the apparel business. As I began to research, and my partner created the designs, I contacted several companies that could print the shirts for me without any luck. However, God provides an opportunity if we are open to accepting.

I contacted a young man who had a screen-printing business in Chicago, Illinois. Our conversation ended with he was too busy to help. However, if I wanted to come to his shop, he could give me pointers on how to get it done. And there was God's opportunity.

I went to the shop, where the young man showed me exactly what he does and what would work best for our designs. That was all it took. Now that I knew what would work, I ordered the equipment, found a t-shirt wholesaler, and we were in business. The designs of those shirts opened so many doors to industries I never imagined I would be in.

We began designing and printing shirts for artists in Hollywood, for stage productions, and for musicians who were going on tour. Sadly, throughout the journey of the first business — although successful and eventful — many mistakes were made and learned from, as failure is only the first attempt in learning.

EXPERIENCE AND EXPERTISE

This leads me to your experience and expertise in the

field you want to start a business in. While it is not uncommon to start a business in an area that you may know nothing about like I did in starting a t-shirt apparel company, it is easier — and better — if you have some knowledge about the industry.

I was once told by a banker that expertise in the field was an essential part of getting a loan. For example, if you wanted to open a dental office, but you were not a dentist, it would be unlikely that the bank would lend you money to start the business. Your experience and expertise lend itself to your credibility and the assurance that you can start and sustain a successful business.

As an entrepreneur, your experience and expertise are what you will draw upon when running your company. The know-how in dealing with customers, employees, and navigating challenging situations is a necessity. Your experience provides you with the ability to handle failure and learn from your mistakes, saving you time and money to focus on acquiring additional skills.

Although some extraordinarily successful entrepreneurs started businesses without experience or formal education, they had the vision, passion, and tenacity to see their dream come alive. As a well-known entrepreneur has said, "Entrepreneurs are not risk-takers. They are calculated risk-takers." As you embark on your journey, remember that entrepreneurs look to lessen the risk at every chance. The difference in risk-takers and calculated risk-takers can be the difference between success or failure.

Questions you might ask: How many years have I worked in this field? Do I know the ins and outs of this product or service? Would I consider myself a subject matter expert in this field?

COMMON MISTAKES MADE

When we start out on this journey, it is common to make mistakes, and some worse than others. Most entrepreneurs start out with limited knowledge of how to actually start a business, let alone run and grow the business. They often get advice from friends, family, other entrepreneurs, and of course, the Internet, where most—if not all—the information is not relevant to their business and is probably wrong.

This brings me to the three most common mistakes made that can cause a business to fail.

No. 1:

The number one mistake entrepreneurs make is over-paying employees. We have all been in situations or jobs where we felt that we just didn't make enough money. Situations like living paycheck to paycheck or even having to get multiple jobs just to make ends meet, often working more than 40 hours a week at your job and not feeling valued because you weren't making enough money. Though we were grateful to have a job at all, we needed more money to make ends meet. This poses problems for entrepreneurs primarily because if you are over-paying employees, it directly impacts the profits of the company.

True story: A friend started a company and started paying his employees just above minimum wage. The employees were doing a great job and sales were going great. Then it happened. An employee begins sharing how they are just barely making it and may have to get a second job. The owner starts to relive his experience of not having enough money to make ends meet and decides to give the employee a significant raise.

This becomes a snowball effect because employees talk to one another. As the owner, you don't want to be perceived as not being fair to everyone. So, you give the next employee the same raise. Eventually, he reaches a point where he is paying out more money than the sales coming in but doesn't notice it right away.

The problem came when the employees lost the motivation to bring in the same number of deals because they would make the same amount of money regardless of how much they sold. Sales began to decrease, but the payroll stayed the same.

This became a massive problem for this entrepreneur because, at this point, he could only afford to pay his employees and not himself. His past experience as an employee made him sympathetic. Understanding they had families, he did not want to lay-off anyone in hopes that sales would once again increase. That was not the case. Because of his emotions and failure to put the business' success first, he had to sell the business in order to avoid losing his home.

If he had only stuck to his original plan of paying the employees based on the revenue goals, adjusted their goals, or found other methods to compensate them for performance rather than across-the-line payroll increases, he would probably still be in business.

Although we may have experienced many situations where we felt that the employer did not understand our worth and we should make more money, as an entrepreneur you must leave those feelings behind. Yes, you can be empathetic and even sympathetic to your employees' situation; however, if your payroll is set based on the projected revenue, you should stick with that. Payroll and payroll taxes is the money going out; it is not money that will bring you a return, such as money invested in a product that will be sold in the business.

I have seen companies where their payroll expense exceeds 65% of their revenue over the past three decades, which means 65% of all the income coming into the company is paid out to payroll. Situations like that make it difficult for a small business to stay afloat. Eventually, they will not be able to meet their other obligations.

No. 2:

The second common mistake is not understanding your market and attempting to start a business without knowing who the competition is. Are you competing with other small businesses, or do the big box stores carry the same product?

Aside from the big box and small businesses, you need to consider online competition as well, such as Amazon and E-bay. The market is changing rapidly, and consumers are looking for the best price for similar products. We would all like to believe that everyone wants and needs our product and service. In theory, it is an excellent thought. In practice, understanding your market base is crucial to the direction of the business.

The reality is that consumers are picky and are often looking for the best deal. Understand your market and customer so that you can compete with others in your market share.

No. 3:

The third most common mistake is hiring employees and paying them as contractors. This mistake is something that I have seen over and over again. It is a violation of labor laws. If caught, the penalty could cause you to lose your company, be fined by the department of revenue and department of employment security, or face imprisonment.

So, let me explain. Entrepreneurs will often bring on an individual and, instead of placing them on payroll, will pay them as an independent contractor. The employer can still write off the expense through a 1099 form at the end of the year, and the employee has to pay his own taxes at the end of the year.

Here is the problem. The definition of an employee is someone who has a scheduled time to work. They have a start and finish time and are not free to come and go as they please. A contractor does not have a schedule; they can come to work when needed and leave when they are done. They are not bound by the rules of the organization. So, employers who try to skirt the payroll tax by paying employees as contractors, if caught, can face many problems.

True story: An entrepreneur in the construction business chose to place only two of the 10 employees on payroll to reduce his workman's comp insurance. The other eight he paid as contractors. Well, every year worker's comp insurance audits the payroll records to determine if the entrepreneur has overpaid or is due a refund. When the records were sent to the auditor, the auditor requested the tax return and discovered that the labor amount was much higher than the projected payroll.

For the entrepreneur to include those employees as contractors, each employee had to have a liability insurance policy for themselves. Thus, the worker's comp did not recognize those eight employees as contractors and charged the entrepreneur with an additional $20,000 in workers' comp fees.

You must ask yourself: is it worth the risk to save a few dollars in the payroll tax? I share these commonly made mistakes to help you recognize issues that could arise.

Think about your business as a child that you are nurturing to grow. You would never do anything to harm your children, so don't take short cuts that can harm your business.

Some additional mistakes are starting a business without a plan, choosing the wrong partner, focusing on growth and not quality, not managing the finances properly, and expanding without proper planning.

In chapter three, we will go over the importance of having a business plan in comparison to working without a plan. But first, let me mention the importance of choosing the right person to partner with.

Often, entrepreneurs will partner with a spouse or significant other, primarily because they want to keep the peace at home. However, this is not always the best idea, especially if both parties are going to be active in daily operations. If you do not have the same business philosophy and entrepreneurial mindset, partnering with the wrong individual will be like an abusive relationship. It could ruin the friendship and/or relationship.

Improper management of finances is another mistake that can bring the business down like a house of cards, as I will cover in chapter six on finances. It is often best to have a financial advisor or accountant to help you in the area of finances.

My philosophy is to stay in your lane. If you are not an accountant or you do not understand finances, then don't do your own business accounting. The same goes for contracts; if you are not a lawyer, then don't write your contracts. You open yourself and the company to errors and liability.

Lastly, expanding without a plan is often a mistake that entrepreneurs make. Lack of proper planning could take down the entire company.

In fact, I know a person who thought that, because his first store was doing so great, the offer to purchase two more stores would increase his revenue. He jumped in without a plan and did not anticipate the problems: lack of sales, employees, and his market. Although he tried and worked tirelessly to run the three stores, he was not financially stable enough to take on that venture so quickly. Ultimately, he had to close and sell the stores at a tremendous financial loss. Have a plan and stick to it.

CHAPTER TWO

Expand Your Idea

The first step to entrepreneurship is the idea. Most of us have a million ideas that we think would make a great and successful business. The idea is to refine the process and find the one you want to use to create a business. There are four steps to refining and making your idea concrete: brainstorming or mind mapping, research, actions, and accountability. A great idea without action is just a great idea.

Let's talk about brainstorming or mind mapping first. If you have a partner, you may want to brainstorm your thoughts; if you are a solopreneur, you may use mind mapping to refine your idea.

BRAINSTORM OR MIND MAPPING

During the brainstorm or mind mapping process, ensure you have something to write all of your ideas on; if you are inviting others to your brainstorming session, use a poster board or whiteboard so that everyone can see and share their thoughts.

Brainstorming or mind mapping is also called brain dumping. It is where you write all of your ideas about your business idea or concept for 5 minutes, then spend the next 5 minutes coming up with questions to answer during research. The last 5 minutes are ideas about marketing and monetizing your idea.

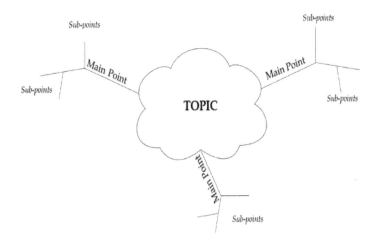

The purpose of brainstorming or mind mapping is to expand your mind and the vision of your business. After completing this exercise, you may find you have a different view of what your business can be, which questions would be necessary to ask, and how to market your business. From the list of ideas generated, you can pick which resonate with you and use them to determine what kind of business you want to create. Not all suggestions made will be kept; in fact, only 5% of the mind mapping thoughts are kept. However, that 5% of insight could provide the direction needed to move forward.

RESEARCH

Step two is research. Once you have your idea, it is essential to research what is already out in the market. Before starting a business or launching a new product or service into a market, it is necessary to conduct a SWOT analysis. A SWOT analysis looks through and discovers the strengths, weaknesses, opportunities, and threats. The internal stance of the company is analyzed when looking at the strengths and weaknesses. The opportunities and threats discovered when looking at the company's viewpoints are external.

The importance of conducting a SWOT analysis is to identify which same or similar products or services are being produced by other companies and how you will differentiate your product or service. Since we are at a starting point, you might look at the SWOT personally. What are your strengths, weaknesses, opportunities, and threats in starting your business?

For example, your strength may be the experience you have in the industry. Similarly, a weakness could be the lack of experience in a field you have never worked in, just like when I chose to start a t-shirt company while never having worked in the apparel or printing industry before. As a result, it took a lot of trial and error to get it going. When looking at opportunities, you may consider how you are going to sell your product or service. Do you already have a large social media following, etc.? As for threats, what is already in the market? Are you competing with big box stores, online retailers, or both?

SWOT ANALYSIS

COMMUNITY

Step three is action. How are you going to find your customers? Many individuals will say if you create a website and social media with a good search engine optimizer (SEO), then the customers will find you. In theory that could be true; however, it's unrealistic. You need to take action to find your customer base.

Ask yourself this: have you ever met someone you knew would be an ideal client because...

- you felt a connection with them right away?

- you knew at your core that you could help them or shared insight that they felt was extremely valuable?

- you spoke their language, and they spoke yours?

Now, ask yourself:

- What are they passionate about?

- What do they struggle with?

- How do they feel at their emotional core?

- What do they want?

- Where may be good places to find them?

Understanding your customer is one of the most powerful things that you can do for yourself and your business. Entrepreneurs will often struggle with defining their customer base because of the fear of putting themselves out there and sharing their own point of view. Society has ingrained in us a culture of wanting or needing to be liked and accepted by others. This is especially true in individuals who wish to make a difference in the community, which causes the need to try to meet the needs of everyone by neglecting their point of view to attract customers.

The importance of having a point of view is that customers align with products that speak to their emotions and validates their point of view. Having a point of view embraces authenticity and makes the customer feel as though you are speaking directly to them. There are three ways you can find your clients: in person, online, or through a partner that already has a client base. You will need to put yourself out there via networking; by attending meetups and community events, the community can get to know and recognize you and your brand.

DEFINING YOUR CUSTOMER AND NICHE

Many entrepreneurs hold themselves back from defining their customer base or niche because they are afraid to get too narrow. Entrepreneurs primarily believe that everyone can benefit from their product or service. The goal is to reach as many people as possible, but the reality is that by not defining your customer, you are unable to specify the market share and end up reaching fewer people. Market research is essential to understanding who is in your market and knowing about the products or services competitors offer, such as their price points and who their clients are.

Narrow down your customer: Who needs you the most?

Write down 5 ideas (categories) of potential customers:

1.
_____

2.
_____

3.
_____

4.
_____

5.
_____

Businesses often appeal to several audiences. Narrowing down the list of customers will help establish your core customers. You can reach several groups, but you will need to adjust your methods for each category.

Once you have established some core groups, you can now drill down and narrow your target market. Your market may be broader than your customer base, but your target customer is within your market.

Skip any questions that do not apply.

1. Is your customer male, female, or both?

2. What age is your target market? (5-year range maximum; up to 3 ranges)

3. What generation tag is your target market? (It can assist in narrowing your research)

4. Where does your target market live? (Is your business local, regional, national, global?)

5. What is the value of their home/condo/apartment? (This may not apply to you)

6. Are they in a corporate job, entrepreneurial, or retired?

7. What is your target market's annual income?

8. Is your target market young families?

9. Is your target market stay-at-home-moms?

10. Is your target market empty nesters?

11. Does your target market have children?

12. Where do your target market's children go to school?

(public or private?)

13. What does your target market do for fun?

14. Does your target market have season tickets to any events? (Theatre? Sports? Concerts?)

15. Where does your target market shop? (Malls or boutiques? Health food or grocery stores?)

16. Where does your target market eat out? (Fast food, local chains, independent five-star?)

17. How often does your target market eat out?

18. Does your target market have help at home?

19. What does your target market do on weekends?

20. Does your target market cook at home? What do they most enjoy preparing?

21. Does your target market take vacations? How Often?

22. Where does your target market go on vacation?

23. What type of hotel/motel is your target market most likely to use?

24. Does your target market have "toys"? (Boats, sports car, luxury sporting goods, etc.)

25. Does your target market drink? If so, how often and what type?

26. Does your target market attend religious services? If so, where?

27. Does your target market lead a healthy lifestyle? If so, what kind of services do they look for?

28. Does your target market care about the environment? Do they recycle?

29. Does your target market follow a political party and agenda?

30. Does your target market belong to an association? What type?

31. What social activities is your target market involved in?

32. Does your target market entertain? How often?

33. Does your target market volunteer?

34. Which charities do they support?

35. What are the TOP 3 financial priorities for your target market?

36. What are your customer members' personal goals?

37. What are your customer members' qualities and personality?

38. What are your customer members' dreams?

39. What are your customer members' values?

40. What are your customer members' problems or concerns?

41. What are your customer members' stresses?

42. What is your customer members' education level?

43. What are your customer members' interests or hobbies?

44. What does your target market: read, wear, spend

money on?

45. How does your target market: socialize, network,

interact?

Questions to ask: Now that you understand your target market, ask yourself how the product or service serves the community? Is the product a want or a need? If you build, will they come?

NAMING YOUR BUSINESS

Coming up with a unique name for your business is often harder than most think. As I worked with entrepreneurs, they would find this task challenging unless they wanted to use some form of their own name. What will be the name of your company? Is it one that is bright, quirky, memorable, matches your Mission or Vision, tells the story without any other words? Some mistakes entrepreneurs make in attempting to come up with a name is they often have too many people involved in making this crucial decision, which can result in a decidedly vanilla or literal name.

Another method used by entrepreneurs is the process of truncation, mixing two adjectives to make a noun such as InstaServ. The adjectives alone are fine, putting them together is like mixing ice cream and barbeque sauce—they don't go well together. Choosing a name by truncation also looks and sounds forced. It is essential to use words that will stand out. Using plain words will not be memorable for the customer. A cleverly crafted name is everything to the business. Many companies have struggled in coming up with an apt name. For example, the Minnesota

Manufacturing and Mining Co. had to evolve their name to 3M and is now known for their innovation.

When choosing the original name for your business, you need to have a clear idea of your brand's personality. What are some words that describe what you do? Who is buying your products or services? There are many methods to creating a company name that represents your brand, personality, and story. Many entrepreneurs use either brainstorming or mind mapping to narrow down the suggestions and identify what their brand will stand for, as well as how consumers will identify with the brand name.

Once you settle on a name you like, you need to protect it. The four ways to register a business name serve different purposes, and some may be legally required based on your business structure and location.

- Entity name protects you at the state level

- Trademark protects you at a federal level

- Doing Business As (DBA) does not provide legal protection but may be legally required

- Domain name protects your business' website address

In the next section, we will cover creating a mission and vision statement for your business, which is something that you may consider when developing your business name.

DEVELOPING A MISSION AND VISION STATEMENT

A vision statement expresses the company's optimal goal and reason for existence. A mission statement provides an overview of the company's plans to realize that vision by identifying the service areas, target audience, and values and goals. However, components of mission and vision statements are often merged to provide a statement of the company's purposes, goals, and values. Sometimes the two terms are used interchangeably. Mission and vision statements can be used both internally and externally.

Internally

- Influences leadership's decision making

- Facilitates performance standards

- Inspires employees to focus and work toward common goals

- Directs employee decision making

- Establishes a structure for ethical behavior

Externally

- Solicits external support

- Establishes a communication link with customers, suppliers, and partners

- Acts as a public relations tool

Below is the organizational planning form that will

help you put all the components together.

Organizational Planning

1. What is the company name?

2. Who are the company's internal and external stakeholders?

Internal stakeholders	External stakeholders

3. Create a company's mission and vision statement

Company's mission

Company's vision

4. Company goals

At least one company goal that can be accomplished through a strategic plan

At least one company goal that can be accomplished through an operational plan

CHAPTER THREE
Create a Road Map

Once you've determined the most appropriate business structure and your company's mission and vision, you will need to develop a business plan. The business plan will be the foundation of your company for years to come. You will revise it often as your company grows, using it as a road map to keep you focused on your goals. A business plan is also useful for raising capital or obtaining loans.

BUSINESS PLAN

The importance of having a business plan is often argued. A study conducted by Tim Berry, founder of Palo Alto Software, provided findings that support the value of creating a business plan. The results of the Palo Alto study stated that 36% of business owners who completed a business plan received a secured loan and secured investment capital, while 64% grew their business. Of those who did not complete a business plan, 18% obtained a loan and investment capital and only 43% grew their business.

IMPORTANCE OF THE BUSINESS PLAN

Developing a business plan is like creating a blueprint for a home or building; without it, construction is impossible.

The sections in a business plan include:

- Executive Summary

- Company Description

- Market Analysis

- Organization & Management

- Product Line or Service

- Marketing & Sales

- Funding Request

- Financial Projections

I know what you're thinking, which is what I thought when I saw the list of items needed in a business plan: *What?! How do I write this? Oh, my goodness, this is so much work. I'll skip this section and move on to what is next in starting a business.* While writing a business plan is not the easiest of things to do, it is essential. If you do not have a plan for your company, where do you start? How do you grow? Ideally, everyone who starts a business is doing so with the intention of growth, success, and profitability.

A solid business plan is necessary if you are looking at obtaining funding or financing. What the business plan does is it shows lenders that you thought out the process of doing business. It talks about the experience you have in the industry. It's a useful tool when trying to convince the bankers to lend you the money.

Business plans come in all shapes and sizes, and there are no firm rules on how to craft them. You can review sample plans in a similar industry, many of which are found online. But in general, business plans contain five main components. An introduction briefly describes your business and its goals, including ownership and legal structure. The plan must highlight your experience and the advantages your company will have over competitors.

Next, a marketing section that identifies the customers' need for your product or service, as well as your market size and location. It also describes your marketing and pricing strategies.

The financial management section should explain how you plan to fund your company and the initial amount of equity capital. Potential investors or lenders will want to see a monthly operating budget and expected return. So, you would need to calculate a projected monthly sales volume, including any expected seasonal trends. This section also describes your businesses' day-to-day operations, including personnel issues, insurance, rental agreements, equipment needs, and anything else relevant to your specific industry. Finally, summarize your goals and objectives while emphasizing your commitment to success.

By this point of the process, you have identified reasons for wanting to start a business and analyzed the market to determine a niche for your product or service. You have also decided what business structure is best suited for your company and have written a comprehensive business plan. Planning a business can be daunting, but it will make you better prepared for when you're the boss. Start small. See results. Grow with results. That's how it's done.

Below is a worksheet to use when developing your road map.

Company Description Worksheet

Business Name	
Company Mission Statement	
Company Philosophy/ Values	
Company Vision	
Goals & Milestones	1. 2. 3.
Target Market	

Industry/ Competitors	1.
	2.
	3.
Legal Structure/ Ownership	

WORKING WITHOUT A PLAN

Working without a plan can lead to an unresolved issue that could influence business failure. More times than not, when a company is just getting started, everyone involved is excited, full of great intentions, and ready to participate in getting it off the ground. You might have second thoughts when others mention hiring a lawyer. Trust me, you need a contract or operating agreement if you are working with potential vendors or sub-contractors.

The lack of contracts or operating agreements can unearth potential problems. Not everyone will see eye-to-eye, and differences will always arise. Once again, *stay in your lane*. If you are not a lawyer, do not write your contracts. From my experience in writing a contract with another individual, I never thought about things such as:

What defined completion? Was it when they gave us the product or when the product is completed without error (quality control)? Did it need to be a certain quality? The agreement included the contractor would receive a percentage of the sale if the company sold, but we never defined what would happen if we fired him or if he quit — would he still get the percentage of the sale? What happens if the product never meets the standard, does that void the contract?

Having a business plan is like being prepared for the road ahead, and a lawyer provides insurance. I would explain the business plan process to my clients as the road map or GPS of the business. It is like asking you to find me in a particular city without giving you the address. How will you locate me? You might arrive in the town, decide to go west, and realize that's the wrong way, so you go south, and that's not it either. That is precisely how business owners who do not have a business plan operate. They go one way and find out that it didn't work, so they go another way, and that didn't work either. It could take them years of mistakes before they figure it out. Having a business plan allows you to control the direction you choose for your business.

ADOPT A PLAN AND PLAN TO ADAPT

Adopt a plan and plan to adapt is about not losing sight of the company's business strategy. Like a GPS, it's okay to make a slight change in direction when necessary, but you need to understand why you're making the change. As I mentioned earlier in the book, it is essential to evaluate what is working and what is not and make the necessary adjustments when starting up.

Some questions you might ask are: Are the company goals going to be achieved in the given timeframe; if not, why? Do deadlines need modification? Determine why you are behind schedule. Did you set realistic goals and action items? Do your goals need to change? Why were the goals not met?

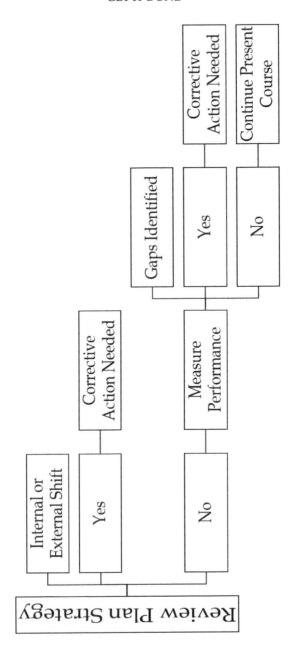

After identifying if the change is needed, implementation is often difficult but necessary. Nonetheless, a company which adopts a plan is ahead of 90% of companies without plans.

SETTING AND DEFINING GOALS

Setting and defining your company's goals are essential to making it happen. Successful companies set goals because there is no focused reason or anything to strive to achieve without them. Goals are the pathway to desired results. A method to set goals is by using SMART goals.

The acronym SMART stands for Specific, Measurable, Achievable, Realistic, and Timely, which is an active process for setting and achieving your business goals. The SMART grid to your goals will help you to create more specific, achievable targets for your business, and to measure your progress toward them. Each goal can have several sub-goals, or actions that need to take place to accomplish the overall goal. The SMART criteria can apply to each of those smaller goals in the same way.

The first letter in the SMART goal acronym is to help you understand what you want to achieve specifically. An excellent way to formulate your specific goal is to think about the who, what, when, where, and why. Who is involved in creating this goal, what do you want to achieve, when do you want to achieve it, where will you achieve it, and why are you achieving it? Be specific in each category.

Second, the goal must be Measurable; determine how

you will measure progress. The measure provides you a method for accessing the goal and verifying that the procedure is tangible and realistic.

Achievable is the A in SMART; this area allows you to ascertain if you have the necessary skill set to achieve the goal or if you need to develop a new skill. The importance of achievable is to identify whether you can make this goal happen.

Fourth is Relevant, which consists of making sure that the goal is in line with your business objectives and focused on your business goals.

Lastly, Time involves setting a specific time frame to achieve the goal, establishing realistic deadlines for the deliverable. A goal without a specific timeframe for completion is less likely to occur because you never solidified the goal with an end time; the goal could drift for months or years without a deadline. Create milestones throughout the timeframe; if the goal is going to take a year to complete, determine what part of the goal should be completed by three months or at the halfway point. Time constraints create a sense of urgency and help you achieve your goals in a timely manner.

For example, set a broad SMART goal for wanting to start a business:

Specific: I will sell my product through Etsy.com.

Measurable: I will be ready to take my first Etsy order within four weeks, and I will aim to sell a minimum of ten items per week.

Attainable: First, I will set up an account on Esty. Then I will build an inventory of 30 items to sell. Lastly, I will promote my business and build customer relationships through word of mouth, referrals, social media, and local networking.

Relevant: Selling my product will allow me to benefit financially.

Time-Based: My Etsy store will be up and running within four weeks, and I will have an inventory of 30 items to sell within six weeks.

CHAPTER FOUR

Establish a Formation

Once you have created your road map, it's time to decide on the type of business formation your business needs. Many times, entrepreneurs want to get into business immediately without concerning themselves with paperwork or with preparation, such as compliance with legal requirements or legal possibilities. By jumping into business without doing various kinds of paperwork, they risk losing opportunities to protect themselves they would otherwise have had. To start, let us first discuss the different business formations along with their advantages and disadvantages.

BUSINESS FORMATIONS

There are various types of business structures for a small business owner to choose from when deciding to start a business. I will cover the sole proprietorship, general and limited liability partnerships, and the types of corporations, including General, Subchapter S, Limited Liability Company (LLC), and Nonprofit.

Sole Proprietorship

The sole proprietor is the individual who starts a business and chooses not to form the company as a partnership or corporation. They may use an assumed name for their business. The sole proprietor is the most accessible formation of a business. With minimal formalities aside from registering an assumed name certificate and gaining a tax identification number, there is no expertise requirement for becoming a sole proprietor. The sole proprietor has full management authority, ease of formation, low cost of the organization, and no double taxation. The sole proprietor has complete control over all business decisions.

One of the disadvantages of the sole proprietorship is it comes with unlimited liability. The owner is solely responsible for all business debt, and lenders will look at both personal and business assets. There is a lack of business continuity if the owners die or cease to do business. More than likely, the company will end. With the lack of diversity in management, a sole proprietor may not have the expertise of others in the business. They may have difficulty in raising capital and problems in transferring the interest of the company.

Partnerships

A partnership is defined as two or more individuals who go into business to make money together. A partnership is formed with an oral or a written partnership agreement. If created by a written agreement, registration with the state is required.

The following elements must be present to constitute a valid partnership:

1. The association of two or more persons, which differentiates a partnership from a sole proprietorship

2. The agreement to carry on as co-owners, which implies that the partnership intends on doing business together

3. The co-ownership part refers to the company being legally owned by more than one person

4. The component of for-profit, referring to the objective of making money in the business (FindLaw, 2008)

The differences between a general partner and a limited partner are that in a general partnership, all partners have equal responsibilities and liability for the business debts and management, whereas a limited partner has limited liability and risk solely to the amount of his/her investment. A limited partner does not have the rights or responsibilities of the daily operation and is not entitled to its management.

Corporations

The various corporation types are general, subchapter S, limited liability company (LLC), and nonprofit. The general corporation is the most common and most complex to form. It is a separate legal entity owned by stockholders that comes with the advantage of the protection of personal assets from business debts or liability. The subchapter S is a general corporation with special Internal Revenue tax status. Subchapter S offers the business owner sole proprietor tax rates.

The limited liability company (LLC) is not a corporation; however, it provides the advantages of a subchapter S corporation, protecting the personal assets from the business debts or liability. The S-corporation and LLC are not taxed — all profit or losses pass-through on the owners' tax returns.

Lastly, nonprofit corporations are formed for civic, charitable, educational, or religious purposes. A nonprofit corporation may be eligible for tax exemption status by defining the nonprofit's use. The nonprofit corporation usually relies heavily on contributions and grants for funding projects and running the corporation. In a not-for-profit corporation, profits carry over to the next year, unlike a corporation or S-corporation where the distribution profit or loss goes to the shareholders. Once you have explored the various types of business formations, you must decide on a business structure that best suits your product or service. If you have chosen a corporation, create the corporation by-laws.

Questions you may need to answer: will you be the sole employee, or will you need to hire others? Will you initially work out of your home, or is there a need to rent or lease space? Does your business have to meet specific codes or regulations? Will you be partnering with someone else? Asking these sorts of questions will help determine the type of business entity that best works for you.

Registering Your Business

Based on the state in which you reside, the secretary of the state handles business registrations. Most states offer an online application and the fees vary according to the type of business formation. You are the registered agent if you are registering the business yourself. However, many entrepreneurs outsource this task to an online legal company such as Rocket lawyer, Swift Filing, and Legal Zoom, to name a few. However, the process is relatively simple and you could save yourself several hundred dollars by doing it yourself.

The secretary of the state will send you the Articles of Incorporation or Articles of Organization once the registration is complete. Now you can file with the IRS for the employer identification number, also known as EIN. This process is straightforward and is completed online at irs.gov by requesting an EIN. Follow the prompts and select receiving the notice online. You will instantly get a PDF version of the letter with your new EIN.

Depending on the type of business formation, you may need to file additional documents with the IRS. For example, if you are an LLC but would like the IRS to classify your business as an S Corp for tax purposes, then you need to file IRS form 2553 within 30 days of starting your business. I would recommend filing immediately after you get your EIN. Most entrepreneurs will forget to register within the timeframe, requiring them to request an exception at tax time.

If your business will sell products or services, you will need to charge sales tax. There is a requirement to apply for a Sales and Use tax number through the state department of revenue. If you are going to pay employees, you need to apply for a withholding tax number as well as an unemployment number from the commission of employment security or unemployment office in your state.

Insurance

Once you have all the required tax identification

numbers, consulting with an insurance agent regarding business liability insurance — and workman's compensation insurance if you have employees — is necessary. Seeking business insurance is essential in protecting you and your company from any potential risk or lawsuit. While an LLC or corporation can protect your personal property from a lawsuit, that protection could be limited. Business insurance helps fill the gap corporate structure does not cover. It can protect your personal and business assets should an unexpected disaster occur.

Specific businesses are required by law to maintain business insurance. For example, the federal government requires every company with employees to have workers' compensation, unemployment, and disability insurance. However, the laws requiring business insurance vary by state, so visit your state's website to determine the requirements. There are different types of insurance that entrepreneurs should have when they start a business. Insurance is the method to mitigate any risk to the company and business owner because one lawsuit or catastrophic event can destroy a small business. There are several types of business insurance, such as Professional Liability, Property, Workers' Compensation, Home-Based, Product Liability, Vehicle, and Business Interruption Insurance.

Professional Liability Insurance

Professional liability insurance is known as errors and omissions (E&O) insurance. It covers a business against claims of negligence that come from failure to perform or from mistakes. However, professional liability insurance is not one-size-fits-all, as the policy is customized based upon the industry.

Property Insurance

Property insurance is a must if the business owns or leases a building or space. Property insurance covers your business equipment, inventory, and furniture should the company suffer loss from natural disasters or theft. However, depending on the state, specified natural disasters are not covered from a standard policy. If your business is in an area that is prone to mass-destruction, such as earthquakes, you may need to acquire a separate policy to cover your business against these events.

Workers' Compensation Insurance

Workers' compensation insurance is a requirement if you are hiring employees and is included in the business insurance policy. Workers' compensation covers medical, disability, and death benefits should an employee get injured or die as a result of his work. For example, if an employee is working in a position that is low risk but slips, falls, and sustains an injury, it could result in an expensive claim against the business.

Home-based Business Insurance

You should consult with your insurance company about attaining a separate policy that will include your business equipment and inventory in the event of a problem. A homeowner's or renters' insurance policy does not offer the same protection of a commercial insurance policy for a home-based business.

Product Liability Insurance

If your business manufactures products, product liability insurance is necessary. Product liability insurance protects your company if the product you manufacture and sell causes injury or damage to the consumer. While the business will take measures to safeguard the consumer from harm, it could happen. For example, if your company manufactures a food product and you fail to disclose an ingredient, there is a risk that a consumer will become ill or die due to a food allergy. Your business could then be liable for negligence because of the overlooked ingredient.

Vehicle Insurance

Vehicle insurance is a must if your business owns vehicles that employees use to deliver products, services, or personnel. In the event of an employee having a car accident while using the company vehicle, the business would be protected from liability. At the very least, the company should acquire third-party injury and comprehensive insurance. You cannot assume that the employee's insurance will cover them in the event of an accident.

Business Interruption Insurance

Business interruption insurance is basically for businesses that have a location such as a retail location. It helps in the event of a disaster that would interrupt business operations. Such an interruption would cause a loss of income resulting from the business's inability to produce the products or service and would prevent employees from working.

Having the right type of insurance for your business is essential to avoid financial loss in the event of a lawsuit or a disastrous occurrence. Generally, as a business owner, any assets and items that you would not be able to replace or pay for on your own should be covered with insurance. It is essential to speak to a licensed insurance agent to identify the type of coverage needed, terms, and prices. It is best to shop around and compare coverage, deductibles, conditions, and cost before deciding.

LOCATION

E-commerce versus brick and mortar, which should you choose? Well, it depends on the type of business you are starting. If you are beginning a product-driven company, then an e-commerce business location would work best. Proper branding and marketing will get you customers from all parts of the world. If your business provides services, such as a spa, it will require a location where customers would need to visit to get the services. However, there are service businesses that are concierge; they go to the customer.

My accounting business is a concierge business. I chose not to have a brick and mortar location to reduce the overhead and decided that I would go to my clients. The accounting I do for small businesses I can do remotely or go to their business. During tax season, I visit my clients at their homes, do their taxes, get paid, and leave. It's efficient, saves time, and is easy for the customer since they have all of their documents at home.

There are also what I like to call hybrid business; they have both brick and mortar and e-commerce sites to extend their reach outside of the local community. We see this in large retail stores such as Target, Kohls, Best Buy, and Walmart, to name a few. I have found that small businesses that have both brick and mortar and e-commerce sites have a difficult time maintaining the e-commerce site. Unless they have a team that works on keeping the site relevant and inventory correct because they are competing with large e-commerce sites like Amazon. The decision is yours to select the best type of location for your business, but remember to understand your market, customers, and competition before making the decision.

CHAPTER FIVE
Build a Brand

Ok, now that we have identified the customer, created plan, and registered a business, how are customers going to find us? It's time to work on building a brand. What do you think of when you hear branding? I thought branding was marketing; however, branding your business is used *in* marketing. Branding is how you identify your business and how your customers recognize and experience your business.

In the previous chapters, we covered defining your customers and writing a mission and vision statement. We set SMART goals to know how and when we will meet specific milestones. Part of that self-discovery journey will help you define your brand. Establishing your brand requires, at the very least, that you answer the questions below:

- What is your company's mission?

- What are the benefits and features of your products or services?

- What do your customers and prospects already think of your company?

- What qualities do you want them to associate with your company?

Since defining a brand can be time-consuming, challenging, and complex, some entrepreneurs seek advice from a brand or marketing expert. However, you may choose to create your brand on your own. Once your brand has been defined, it's time to introduce it to the world. How? Here are a few ways to launch your brand:

• Get a logo that represents your brand and place it everywhere. If you are not a graphic designer, hire a designer to create your company logo. You want to make sure that you have the highest quality in all the formats available for online and print in high resolution.

• Determine your brand message, the key message you want to communicate about your brand, and write it down.

• Integrate your brand into every aspect of the business, from how employees answer the phone to what your employees wear to signatures on emails.

• Give your brand a voice. Is it formal? Is it friendly? Communicate this voice through all the media channels, in print and online.

• Develop a tagline, something that is memorable and captures the essence of the brand.

• Create brand standards; colors, themes, fonts, look, and feel should be consistent.

• Be true to your brand.

Being consistent is crucial in order to keep the customers returning.

WEBSITE AND DOMAIN NAME

First, let's talk about the domain name. The domain name is the "foundation" for the brand. A domain name identifies your company on the internet. There are so many extensions from which to choose (.com, .org, .net, etc.), but the most common are .com and .org.

Choosing your domain name can be a daunting task. Oftentimes, the name you choose for your company may not be available in the domain name, as someone else may already own it. In that case, you would need to find an acronym that will represent your company name. Regardless of whether you are an existing company or just starting, you need to have a strong online presence. Most consumers, when searching for a product, will explore the internet to either find the product in their local area or find the product that can be purchased online and shipped to them directly. If your company website is easy to find and navigate, it will increase your chance of a sale.

Most consumers conduct their shopping or product research online. With the dynamic change in marketing, a well-developed and maintained website provides the potential for a vast reach of customers. With the right domain name, you can create a lasting brand image. The domain name decision should not be made in haste. Remember, it is the most valuable marketing tool your company has that will lead customers to your site. It could be the most crucial decision you make when etching out your portion of the online market.

A well-crafted domain can add professional credibility to your business. It provides visibility for your brand, establishes your business as forward-thinking, creates mobility for your internet presence, and provides brand marketability worldwide. Consumers are also cautious when purchasing from someone who may advertise their product on social media but does not have a website. The consumer will research the business before buying. If there is no website with a consistent message, they may think it is a scam and not purchase. Professional credibility is essential to gain the consumers' trust, as consumers only buy from those they trust. A solid domain space is a start to establishing your credibility.

You should try to create a domain name that is short and easy to remember, one that is ideally six to ten letters. Simple, concise, and typeable. The longer the title, the higher the chance for misspelling and typos. Avoid using hyphens and numbers, as they complicate the user's ability to find you. Remember, the more accessible it is for the customer to find your business online, the better.

A powerful domain name is essential regardless of the size of the company. A smart slogan or title will entice customers. It should differentiate your business from others in your industry. Just like you did when you decided on the type of logo for your company, selecting a domain name should reflect your brand. It should be memorable and straightforward.

EMAIL

Email accounts are another way that shows the

customer you are a credible business. I must say that many small businesses chose to skip this and use Gmail accounts for their business. The customer will wonder if this is a real or credible business, or if it is someone working out of their home. They will ask themselves if they trust the shop to purchase the item online. An email account with your company name as the extension shows the consumer you are a legitimate company; it provides professional credibility and legitimacy. If you do not want to use your name in the email, use info@yourcompany.com or sales@yourcompany.com.

You will find that customer, vendor, investor, banker, etc. will take your business more seriously when responding with an email that has your company extension. Typically, when you purchase your domain name, you will have the option to acquire your company email.

WEBSITE HOSTING

Now that you have a domain name and an email, you need to decide who will host your domain or create your website to begin developing your online presence. There are various website hosting companies and types of hosting, depending on how robust your website will be. Are you creating an e-commerce site with an online store? A website can also be customized to give the clients the ability to book appointments for services and can provide information about your store's product and location.

Questions to ask yourself: Do I want to build the site on my own? Should I hire an expert to create my website? What information do I want the world to know about my business? Am I going to sell products online or just provide information? Do I want customers to schedule appointments? Do I want to have a blog on my site? How can I create a client database on my website?

To ensure the brand message and voice are consistent, you should write out each page's content. Companies like WIX, Shopify, Squarespace, and GoDaddy, to name a few, make it extremely easy to build a website, purchase a domain, set up an email account, and offer real-time editing. However, if you are unclear about your message and your brand voice, a poorly created site could keep customers away. If using a hosting service, you will have the option of purchasing your domain and email for one to five years. My recommendation is to commit to five years. Paying for it upfront will make it one less concern in the future.

Many entrepreneurs purchase for one year and forget to renew. Guess what happens? They end up losing their domain name, and the site goes down. If you have built a significant online presence, this could be disastrous. Your customers will no longer be able to find you and may think you have gone out of business or closed. Prevent that error from happening and purchase the five years.

SOCIAL MEDIA

Social media is a vital part of your marketing plan and strategy. Social media platforms like Facebook, Instagram, Twitter, and LinkedIn are ways to help you connect with your customers and build brand awareness. The right social media message will improve leads and sales, as well as create a following that will lead to recurring customers and referrals. The fantastic growth that social media provides to businesses is something that each small business should leverage in the best way possible. If your target customer is out there on social media engaging with their favorite brands, you want them to engage with your brand as well. Statistics show that customers who had positive experiences with a brand will recommend the brands on social media accounts, will become a recurring customer, and are more likely to share a direct link to your company website. Harness this great aspect of social media; the effect it can have on your brand and business can make all the difference.

So, let's talk about the small business owner who doesn't know anything about social media, how to set up the account correctly, how to interact with customers, or how to keep it relevant. In my experience, everyone tells the small business owner, *"you have to be on social media for customers to find you."* In part, this is true. However, most of the entrepreneurs I have encountered can set up a social media account on Facebook or Twitter, but do not have the time to keep it relevant; to post, respond, and engage with customers daily. They do not know how to schedule posts or set up events or campaigns that would let the consumer know about any new items or relevant business updates. Setting up a social media account is easy. Keeping it relevant and current is more tasking, especially when you are trying to run your business. It takes time and work to make sure your brand voice is consistent and relevant to what is happening in your business.

If you are not an expert on social media, find someone to help you manage your social media account. Often, entrepreneurs will intern a college student who may be studying marketing to help with the set up and maintenance. In return, they offer proof for college credit. Remember, where there is good there is also bad. Social media can destroy a brand if a customer has a bad experience. The customer can effortlessly post on social media and share the bad experience, negatively influencing their followers along with your potential customers.

True story: A customer went to one of my clients' shop to have some work done on his vehicle. When the customer returned to pick up his truck, he claimed an item from the interior went missing. My client had security cameras in the shop. The client reviewed the cameras and found that nothing had been removed from the inside of the vehicle. Although my client did nothing wrong, it did not stop the customer from slamming them all over social media. He called them thieves and filed a police report to find out through the police investigation that the customer's son had removed the item from the vehicle before he took it to the shop. But the damage was done. That comment prevented other customers from coming to the business, and when customers would call the shop, they would ask if the theft occurred.

The impact of social media can be significant when it's positive. Still, it can also be very damaging if there is something negative. Tread cautiously and ensure that your brand meets your mission and vision; that all your content is consistent and you provide excellent service. It is challenging to overcome negative information on social media. Whenever a person searches for reviews, it will be there. There may be hundreds of positive reviews and comments, but one negative can overshadow them all.

MARKETING

Marketing is putting together everything we have previously talked about and pushing your brand across a variety of platforms. First, get organized. After the various tasks up to this point, you should have a clear and concise message about your brand, which is often called an elevator pitch. You should be able to let your customer know about your business, product, or service in 30 seconds or less. Second, launch your company website to leverage your social media.

Create local awareness by networking, sponsoring an event, and offering give-away SWAGG (promotional items with your company logo, name, and contact information). Create customer loyalty by offering coupons or free products or services. Find a brand ambassador to create a buzz around your brand and advertising. Keep in mind, advertising is not one size fits all.

There are different advertising methods. Make sure you pick the one that works best for you and will bring in the best return on your investment (ROI). Remember, customers need to hear about your brand at least seven times before they act. Optimize all platforms available for target customers to reach you and you will in turn be better able to reach *them*.

COPYRIGHT OR TRADEMARK

What is a trademark?

A trademark is a word, phrase, symbol, or design—or a combination thereof—that is used to differentiate one company from others working in the same field of business and offering the same products or services. Registering and acquiring a trademark gives notice to other companies that your company name, logo, and products are exclusively your property, giving you the exclusive right to use them in connection with your services or products.

What is copyright?

Copyright protects original work, such as books, songs, photography, and other original work of an author expressed in physical form. According to the United States Copyright Office, copyright protects original works such as "literary, dramatic, musical, artistic and certain other intellectual works." It's important to note that original work is copyrighted the moment its created. However, the protection from infringement comes with registering the original work to prevent others from using it. The registration provides evidence of original work in the case that another person or company steals it.

Most entrepreneurs never think about or consider the need to copyright or trademark their brand logo or name. The general rule is if your business operates in one state and does not plan to extend to work in other states, a trademark is not necessary. You already have the right to use your company name and brand by registering your company within the state. However, whether you choose to extend to other states, then a trademark eliminates the confusion of another company using the same name or logo, especially if you plan to have a significant online presence.

Your company logo reflects your niche and brand personality; it is the DNA of your brand and business, so applying for copyright or trademark is an important decision. It safeguards against losing rights if another company uses the same or similar name.

Once you place your logo on the company website, you may want to consider copyrighting and trademarking the logo and name to prevent others' copyright infringement. The copyright and trademark ensure that you secure your intellectual property and prevent another company from stealing your original ideas and brand logo. The great thing is that trademarks never expire if you are using your trademark in commerce to identify your product or service.

There are several ways to apply for a copyright or trademark. The application process through the United States Patent and Trademark Office and the United States Copyright Office can be overly complicated. Both applications are available online, and the application processing time can take from 8 to 13 months. There are several ways you can go about filing a copyright or trademark application. Companies such as the Trademark Engine can submit your application and monitor its progress to ensure the application is completed without error.

Another option is hiring an attorney that handles patents, trademarks, and copyrights. This alternative can be costly. You can also use an online attorney found on companies like Legal Zoom or Rocket Lawyer to file the trademark application. Regardless of which path you choose to utilize in obtaining a copyright or trademark for your brand, make sure that you shop around and find the best fit for you and your brand.

CHAPTER SIX

Understand Your Finances

This section is the biggest potential downfall for entrepreneurs. As an emerging entrepreneur, you will need to look at your financial skills realistically. Starting and operating a business takes planning, as well as a significant emotional and financial commitment. Unfortunately, the odds are not always in your favor.

According to the American Factfinder, 22% of female and 3% of male entrepreneurs fail each year. The saying "people don't plan to fail; they fail to plan" rings true when it comes to entrepreneurial success.

The importance of managing your business' finances is vital to its success. Entrepreneurs who do not have a lot of experience managing finances can view it as a difficult task and can potentially fall into creating bad financial habits.

Entrepreneurs must educate themselves on the necessary skills in finance, like the basics of accounting, how to create and understand financial statements, applying for funding, and how to organize finances. As an accountant, there is nothing more frustrating than when a client shows up with boxes of receipts and/or bank statements from the entire year to close the year and complete their tax returns. How do you, as the entrepreneur, even know if your business is making or losing money if you are not organized and able to track the profit or loss monthly? I cannot overstate the importance of accurately tracking your company's financial information throughout the year, not just at the end of it.

There are a few key points to consider when organizing your business finances.

First, you should pay yourself. When first starting out, entrepreneurs will often fail to pay themselves because they feel that the company needs the capital. Similar to the story I told earlier, where the business owner paid everyone except himself and overpaid his employees to the point of almost losing his home, If you do not pay yourself and the company does not work out, you will have worked the entire year for free and could run the risk of losing more than just your business.

Second, depending on the type of business you start, having a sound billing system in place allows you to manage the daily operations and cash flow. If you have a difficult time collecting from customers, then you may need to find a more creative way to collect. A possibility would be changing terms and offering a discount if they pay in full or before the due date, such as 2/10 net 30. This means that if they pay in full before the 10th day, they receive a 2 percent discount; otherwise, the entire balance is due in 30 days.

Third, set aside time to review and monitor your books. Even if you are using an accountant or bookkeeper, you will be familiar with your business finance and better able to prevent any potential financial crime. Establishing financial procedures can go a long way in helping you to mitigate risk and potential fraud.

Lastly, plan. Business issues are inevitable. When it comes to finances, you need to prepare for the future, look at methods to invest in future growth, and set money aside for those potential opportunities. A small business that wants to grow and innovate will attract better employees and create value for your company. However, as I have said throughout, remember to *stay in your lane.* If you are not an expert in finance or accounting, then find an accountant to assist you with your finances.

BANKING

One of your first tasks is to establish a business bank account after registering and receiving the EIN. However, there are a few things you should know. When you go to the bank to set up your account, they will ask for your articles of organization or incorporation and proof of your EIN. If you have a partnership or corporation, they may ask for the meeting minutes that provide you permission to open the account at that specific bank.

The banker will also ask for the owner's or corporate officers' personal information to create a profile and link it to the company. This is where you want to ensure that the account is not linked to your profile and social security number but the company's EIN.

More times than not, the banker will link the account to the owners' social but place the EIN in the profile. It could provide the appearance of co-mingling funds, which is a violation and could cause a loss of corporate protection. If the bank account has a debit or credit card, it is vital to make sure that it is linked to the company EIN and not the owners' social. Incorrect linking is a common mistake made by bankers who issue debit or credit cards to owners and corporate officers. Although the card will have the company name, the card is linked to the individual's profile and not the company's profile.

The purpose of an incorporation is to separate personal assets from business assets and reduce the liability of losing personal assets if there was a lawsuit. If your bank accounts give the appearance that you are using personal assets for business purposes, the separation of assets is eliminated. If you get sued, you could lose not only your business but your personal assets as well.

CREDIT

That brings me to credit. Most entrepreneurs do not know the difference between business credit and personal credit. Most individuals know that personal credit based on the accounts created personally are reported to the three major credit bureaus: TransUnion, Equifax, and Experian. The reported personal score is based on a FICO scoring system, which is 0 – 900. With business, there is a separate business credit scoring system and business credit bureaus (Dun & Bradstreet, Business Equifax, Business Experian).

The scoring is called Paydex and is based on how you pay your business accounts in comparison to others in the same industry. Put simply, a Paydex score is a credit score for businesses. These exclusive scores are generated by Dun & Bradstreet (D&B), with possible Paydex scores ranging from 1 to 100. A score of 90 or higher indicates an excellent payment history, and a score below 80 indicates that your bills were paid late. The score is also dollar-weighted, which means the bigger the bill, the more "weight" it will have on your score.

Establishing business credit is essential to the growth of your company. Ensure that your vendors are reporting to the business credit bureaus. If they are tied to your profile and social security and they are only reporting to your personal credit, it will not help your business in any way.

FUNDING

An especially important part of planning how to start your company is deciding how you are going to fund your business. Most entrepreneurs self-fund and use their personal money to start; they may take funds from savings or their 401K retirement account. The second method is turning to friends and family for funds. The third method is using personal credit (credit cards, lines of credit) against personal property. Lastly, one can apply for loans.

So, let's talk about self-funding, or using your personal or credit card money to start. The problem with self-funding is that the funds will eventually run out before you start to make a profit. If you did not keep track of the money you personally put into the company, you will never recover that money. Secondly, when the money runs out, you may turn to friends or family to assist. If they believe in your company, they may lend you the money to help you get going. The big sources are loans and lines of credit. If you own a home, you may decide to take a line of credit against your property as collateral. Big mistake! Do not borrow against your property as collateral for a business loan. Should something happen to the business, the bank could make you sell the home for the remaining balance of the loan. If the value of the house goes down in a time of a recession, the bank could act against you to recover the deficiency in the loan amount.

New entrepreneurs without business credit have a difficult time getting loans and lines of credit. Because the company does not have credit, it has not proven to the bank that it pays its debts on time. It is possible that the bank may offer a loan or line of credit with a personal guarantee if the owner or officer has good credit. A personal guarantee means that you are personally guaranteeing that the company will pay the loan or line of credit based on the bank's terms. If the company defaults, the bank will hold you personally liable for the loan.

Additionally, loans with personal guarantee are just personal loans used for business; they do not report to the business credit bureaus. They report to the personal credit bureaus, which will lower your credit score because the debt to income ratio is significantly increased. When entrepreneurs with no established business credit apply for a loan and do not want to agree to a personal guarantee, bankers will require a minimum of two years of profitable tax returns before providing a loan exclusively on the business. Oftentimes entrepreneurs become desperate and turn to high-interest loans for quick and fast money. Loans that offer quick money come at a high cost, with interest rates as high as 63% or higher. They end up costing the company thousands of dollars in interest. Those high-interest lenders entice new entrepreneurs because they know that the traditional banks are not going to lend them money.

They structure those loans as merchant cash advances, where they take a percent of the credit card sales daily or draft the company account daily. Well, $200 a day or $500 a day at the moment of desperation may not seem so bad. But looking at it on a monthly basis, $200 a day is equal to a $6,000 per month loan payment and $500 daily becomes $15,000 per month loan payment where 63% of that payment covers interest alone. My advice is to resist any type of quick and fast money because it will put you in a hole that will be exceedingly difficult to climb out of.

When lenders review the loan application, they are looking at what is commonly known as the five C's of lending: character, capacity, capital, conditions, and collateral.

Character is the Business' Credit and Payment History:

- Business' credit scores, payment history, education, work history, etc.

- Business' stability, reliability, credibility, relationship with lenders.

Capacity is the Business' Income and Cash Flow:

- Business' cash flow, income, profits, revenue, and so on for each month.

- Business guarantees the ability to pay back the lender.

Capital is the Business' Savings and Investments:

- Business' savings, money for investments, down payments, etc.

- Business' investment returns, retirement, emergency funds, etc.

Conditions is Business' Purpose and Situations:

- Business' circumstances, economy, market, education, ability, etc.

- Business' industry, experience, competition, the purpose of the request.

Collateral is the Business' Assets and Resources:

- Business' assets, equipment, real estate, inventory, vehicles, etc.

- Business' homes, rentals, account receivables, cash, security, etc.

True story: a customer who had been in business for one year went to the bank to get a loan for operating expenses and did not want a personal guarantee. The banker tells him he needs two years of profitable tax returns. The customer is told to return next year. He makes it to year two and goes back to the banker. Still, with no established business credit, the banker tells him he hasn't shown a significant year-over-year profit and to come back next year.

The tradelines the customer was using were not reporting to the business credit bureaus. Most were tied to his personal profile without him having any idea that those lines were not helping his business. In the meantime, the customer was desperate for funding, so he turned to high-interest loans. It was quick and fast, but quick and fast can take your company down faster. This situation went on for more than five years before he finally had to give in and sign a personal guarantee to get out of the debt he had placed the company in.

He realized that the reason he could not get funding from the bank exclusively based on the business was because he did not have the components that met the five C's of lending. The largest was the lack of business credit established. He began building business credit, and there it was: the availability to capital, loans, and a credit card based on the company without a personal guarantee.

INVESTORS

Entrepreneurs or start-ups will often ask if they need an investor. Before covering the types of investors, let's first define what an investor is. An investor is a person or entity who commits financial backing with the expectation of financial returns. There are different types of investors, and we covered the first few in the funding section.

Investor types include:

- Family and Friends

- Banks

- Angel Investors

- Venture Capitalist

- Corporate Investors

The investment source previously covered, family and friends, is the first one entrepreneurs will approach when they need capital to get their business started. However, these types of investors rarely provide a lot of money. Their investment could range from $1000 to $100,000.

Another investment source mentioned was going to the bank for a loan or line of credit. These loans are provided based on the entrepreneur's profile because the business does not yet have credit or assets to act as collateral to secure the loan or line.

Next, there are Angel Investors, wealthy individuals who invest their money into start-up companies in exchange for convertible debt or owners' equity. Angel Groups are groups of Angel investors who pool their money to invest in start-up companies, which helps in mitigating risk and promotes the willingness to invest larger amounts individually.

Then there are the Venture Capitalists, who are the opposite of Angel investors. The Venture Capitalist investor is a firm investing other people's money that is held in a fund. Venture Capitalists (VCs) are considered the holy grail of fundraising. They come with the most substantial checks, power, and the ability to secure the market share, credibility, and visibility.

Lastly, Corporate Investors are corporations that invest in start-ups. They provide capital, expertise, or access to distribution *channels. A corporate investor can become an important customer or supplier for the new business, and the corporation's willingness to invest can provide an important endorsement for the new business.*

There are advantages and disadvantages to each type of investor. Starting and operating a small business comes with risk; having an investor who shares that risk can help reduce the chances of financial failure. Investors typically expect to be involved in the operations of the business to protect their investment. However, the advantage of combining talents and skills can lead to business success.

Keep in mind, having investors does come with some disadvantages, one of which is the loss of control of the business. The more significant the investment, the more right the investor has in asserting control in the decision-making process and daily operations. Additionally, some investors find it challenging to invest in small businesses because of the limited return potential, which means you may need several investors.

The more investors you have, the more individuals you need to report to, which takes away from the planning, operating, and focusing on the businesses' bottom line. Most importantly, you need to precisely analyze what you are willing to give away before you set out to find an investor.

UNDERSTAND YOUR FINANCES

True story: A person I know is an inventor and had created an amazing product. He received a patent and was looking at the next steps in creating a prototype and how to get the product to market. He shared his idea with another friend, who offered to give him $10,000 dollars for 30% return on investment (ROI). Not knowing what that investment would mean financially and only thinking about needing money to get his prototype created and marketed, he almost said yes.

Then I get the phone call, where he begins to explain what he is doing and what the person is offering. I quickly said absolutely not. I explained that he was going to need far more than $10,000 to get this product to market.

Then I asked, are you willing to give up 30% of your companies' profits for a $10,000 investment? That is absurd. Just imagine your company making a million dollars net in the first year and giving up 30% for that initial $10,000 investment.

UNDERSTAND RETURN ON INVESTMENT (ROI)

Understanding return on investment (ROI) is essential to making effective decisions about investing in a product or service, as well as deciding if and when you might seek an investor. ROI seems like a complicated financial term; however, it is straightforward. ROI is a ratio between the investment and the return.

ROI = (Return – Investment)

Investment

Investments that generate small returns are not desirable. For example, should you decide to take out an advertisement in a local magazine, the cost is $400. Though you may think it's not a lot of money, the advertisement generates $100 in additional profit— not a good investment, as the cost was $300 more than the return. Even if it generated $400 and you broke even, it still would be a bad investment. The key to investment is to get a good rate of return. An investment of $500 that generates a $2000 return would be a better investment.

A common mistake made when calculating ROI is that entrepreneurs will look at the additional sales dollars generated by the investment without removing the cost of goods sold. They are looking at the gross profit and not the net profit. We can take the same scenario from above as an example: if the advertisement cost $400 and generated $600 in additional sales, you might initially think this is good. In reality, when you remove the cost of goods of $400, the advertisement generated $200 in profit, and a $200 return on a $400 investment is not good.

Most of us have heard of the show shark tank, where entrepreneurs pitch their ideas or existing businesses to experts in hopes that one of the experts will invest in their company.

The advantage of Shark Tank experts is the exposure to everyone watching on television. Every viewer will hear of the business or product. It also adds the expertise, knowledge, and experience of the expert when launching the business or turning it around. It provides the vast network the expert has to the distribution, marketing, and production that can make the business successful and profitable.

Of course, the investors are expecting a significant return on their investment and, more often than not, they will own the majority share in — and control of — the company. It is almost as though you went from entrepreneur to employee because you no longer hold a controlling share of the business.

However, the most obvious is that with that type of investment comes wealth. Not only is the investor making a substantial ROI, but you as the entrepreneur are also making a lot of money.

ACCOUNTING

Accounting and recordkeeping are vital to your business. As the entrepreneur, a part of managing your finances is knowing what the revenue, expenses, and liabilities are monthly. Having a clear picture of what you owe and who owes you allows you to maintain control. Now, as I have mentioned earlier, I stand by the idea that if you are not an accountant or bookkeeper, you should hire and use an accountant or bookkeeper.

However, there is self-help accounting software that can provide great assistance in keeping your finances organized, such as QuickBooks, Xero, and FreshBooks. These services also offer live bookkeepers to oversee your entries at an additional cost.

Additionally, these programs offer payroll services, worker's compensation, invoicing, and online payments to help keep your finances organized and all in one place. If you choose a self-help accounting method, I suggest using an accountant quarterly in order to ensure that your books are balanced and reconciled, and that all liabilities are paid correctly. Additionally, the accountant can prepare your financial statements and explain how to read them. They can provide advice on trends that are occurring along with changes you might consider, information you otherwise may not have known about. The objective is to keep your finances organized while looking for methods that can streamline expenses, thus continue to grow your business.

CHAPTER SEVEN

Develop Human Capital

Building a plan, identifying your customer, understanding finance, and creating a brand are all important parts of entrepreneurship. However, human capital can be an entrepreneur's greatest asset. The employees you hire will come with a vast amount of knowledge and experience. The additional training you provide in your company on the product or services will assist in making that employee an expert in your company.

Knowing how to hire employees is essential if you are going to do the screening. Entrepreneurs will often start their companies while being the only employee working on getting the company off the ground. This decision is made because of a lack of capital. However, if you are trying to sell your product or service, when will you have time to also grow your company, identify what the competition is doing, and maintain your social media and website presence? You won't. Hiring someone to help with the business' daily operations will allow you to focus on running and growing your business.

HIRING EMPLOYEES

There are several methods to find prospective employees with the experience and expertise you need for your business. There are online job posting sites, such as Indeed, Monster, and ZipRecruiter. As the employer, you can post your position on the online forum and review resumes and applications as they are submitted. You can post the position on social media and drive the individual to your website to apply for the job. Or, you can put a sign in your store window if you have a brick and mortar location.

You can also hire a recruiting company that specializes in your business needs to assist in finding candidates. The recruiting agency will screen each candidate, make sure they meet your minimum qualification, background check the candidate, set up the interview, and offer the employment should you decide to hire.

Of course, hiring a recruiting agency to find your candidates will bring with it a cost. However, the cost may be worth the investment to get a person who can help grow your business with sales because they have a proven track record. The lower-cost methods will come from posting on online job boards, but you will have to do all the work: create the job posting, review and pre-screen all the applicants, set up the interview, conduct a background check, and offer the position. The choice is based upon your need and the minimum qualifications of the individual you are attempting to hire. The more complex the need, the harder it is to find qualified candidates on your own.

RECORDKEEPING

As an entrepreneur, it is your responsibility to ensure that your employees are legally eligible to work in the country of origin. Determining eligibility is through the verification of required paperwork and documents.

DEVELOP HUMAN CAPITAL

Before the first date of employment, the new hire should complete the forms for payroll withholding and the employment eligibility verification form I9 from the US Citizenship and Immigration Services. The employee will need to provide a copy of government-issued identification and a social security number. The employer will sign the I9 form that they have seen, copied, and verified for authenticity.

As an entrepreneur, you will keep these forms in a file for each employee. Employers can also use E-Verify to validate that the documents presented by the employee are authentic. This process eliminates the hiring of employees who have committed identity theft and are using someone else's social security for employment purposes.

True story: a client hired an employee with all the correct documents, identification, and social security card and filled out all the hiring forms. The employer did not think it was necessary to use the E-Verify service because he thought the employee was legitimate. After about a year, he received a letter from the IRS questioning the employment of the employee, because the social security used belonged to a person who was collecting social security retirement.

Social security wanted to verify that this person was working and earning a wage. The person who the social security belonged to was being investigated. Social security was going to cancel his social security payments because he was earning more than allowed.

We all want to believe that every person we hire is honest and that their intention is correct. Still, it is your duty and responsibility to protect your company. Verify everyone, even if you think it's a waste of time.

EMPLOYEE VERSUS CONTRACTOR

Employee versus contractor is a topic that I discuss with each of my clients, and there are some legal consequences of getting it wrong. So, let us begin by defining what constitutes a person as an employee. According to the Internal Revenue Service, the legal definition of an employee is "a person usually below the executive level who is hired by another to perform a service especially for wages or salary and is under the other's control."

In basic English, an employee is a person hired to work a specific number of hours full-time or part-time for a wage; they clock in and out. They do not have the control to come and go as they please throughout the workday without asking for the employers' permission. For example, you work 8 hours per day; as an employee, you can't just say you're done for the day after 3 hours and go home without the employer's permission. The employer controls the hours worked and pay received.

A contractor is hired to conduct the same or similar jobs as the employee, but is not under the employer's financial control. They are hired to complete a specific task or job and get paid based on the completion of the task or job. They work as required and do not have a set schedule for arriving and leaving, unless the employment contract states they are to work during a specific time frame.

DEVELOP HUMAN CAPITAL

Most independent contractors are just that: independent. They show up based on their schedule and leave when done. They may be working for several clients and allocate their day based on the clients they need to visit on a specific day.

Whether to hire an employee versus a contractor is where it gets messy. Be cautious of how you classify those you hire.

Why, you ask? As an employer, it is your obligation to pay the employers' share of withholding taxes for social security, unemployment, Medicare, and pay worker's compensation insurance on the individuals that work within your organization. Sometimes an employer might choose to classify an employee as an independent contractor, a decision that can bring with it many consequences. It denies the employee from benefits and protections of which they are legally entitled to, such as minimum wage, overtime compensation, family and medical leave, and unemployment compensation.

Entrepreneurs who misclassify the employee as contractors believe that it reduces their employer liabilities and ultimately saves them money by keeping payroll cost down.

However, the consequences of misclassification are steep. According to the IRS, they come with penalties, criminal convictions, and even jail time. It also opens the employee to a federal and state audit for wages received as an independent contractor. The IRS will demand that any business deductions taken on taxes are returned.

In addition, the Department of Labor will require they pay taxes on the back wages for up to three years and will levy fines and penalties if they uncover a violation of wage and hours reported.

On top of that, the state unemployment and worker's compensation will require back payments of unemployment insurance and worker's compensation premiums, including levying fines and penalties for lack of reporting or recordkeeping.

So, I would suggest that you consider the classification carefully before paying them as an independent contractor to reduce your employer liability. Often, the employee will ask you to pay him as a 1099 contractor because of personal reasons, such as trying to avoid being subjected to a wage garnishment for child support. The employee is trying to evade their responsibility, and that is not your concern as the employer. It is your responsibility to follow the laws of your state.

Are you willing to go to jail and pay fines — or lose your company entirely — in order to help an employee evade their responsibility and avoid a wage garnishment? Most would say, no way! But from my experience, many have. It goes back to the story at the beginning about the employer who sympathized with the employee's situation. Even if you have been there before, please don't do it; it will cost you more than you know.

CHAPTER EIGHT

Know About Taxes & Tax Returns

Now that we have covered planning and building your business, taxes is an area that many entrepreneurs know little about and can negatively impact the business and business owners if done incorrectly. As an entrepreneur, it is essential that you are aware of the various types of taxes that your business is required to file. According to the Internal Revenue Service, the general types of business taxes are income, estimated, self-employment, employment, and sales tax.

First, let's discuss income tax. This tax is best known for the tax that is withheld from employees and is paid as the employee earns income throughout the year. If not enough, tax is withheld from the earned income to satisfy the individuals' tax liability. They may be required to pay estimated tax or pay income tax when they file their annual tax return.

Second, entrepreneurs and some self-employed individuals are required to pay estimated tax through the year. Typically, an accountant will forecast the year's earnings and determine the estimated tax due at the end of the year and divide the tax amount into four quarterly tax payments. Estimated tax is used to pay income tax, self-employment tax, and alternative minimum tax. Paying estimated taxes prevents the entrepreneur or self-employed individual from paying the total tax due at the end of the year when they file their tax return.

Businesses which include sole proprietors, partners, and S corporation shareholder are expected to owe tax of $1000 or more when they file their tax return. They are all expected to make estimated tax payments. Corporations are expected to pay estimated taxes if their tax owed is $500 or more. Generally, the Internal Revenue Service states that you may have to pay estimated tax if your prior-year tax owed was greater than zero.

The third tax category is self-employment tax, which is a social security and Medicare tax for those who are self-employed. Generally, the self-employed will pay self-employment tax if they receive net earnings of more than $400. The self-employment tax contributes to the entrepreneur's coverage under the social security system. Social security coverage provides benefits for retirement, disability, survivor, and Medicare hospital benefits.

The fourth tax type is an employment tax. This type of tax is the employers' obligation when they have employees. The employer has the responsibility to file and pay social security and Medicare tax, federal income tax withholding, and federal unemployment (FUTA) tax. Most entrepreneurs will use payroll systems such as QuickBooks payroll, Gusto, Paychecks, or ADP, to name a few, in order to take care of their payroll needs, ensuring that all payroll taxes are withheld. Employer tax obligations should be filed and paid in a timely manner. Payroll tax is an area that can cause employers to get in trouble. The failure to pay taxes withheld or the employers' portion of tax due will add penalties and interest to the amount of tax due.

Lastly, sales tax is required to collect and pay on sales of products and services. If you sell a product, whether online or in a retail brick and mortar store, you are required to charge and collect sales tax on every sale. The timing of when sales tax returns are filed depends on the location of your business. However, most states require payment of sales tax to the department of revenue by the 20th day preceding the closing month. For example, taxes due for January is due by February 20th. Business taxes are complicated, and my advice is to seek guidance from an accountant or tax professional to ensure that you are prepared and that you understand the various tax filings. You will need to establish an account with the Electronic Federal Tax Payment System (EFTPS) to pay withholding taxes electronically. A separate account with your state department of revenue is created to pay the sales tax collected.

Tax Returns

As we covered in chapter three, the various types of business formations also have different types of tax obligations and tax returns that need to be filed. The tax cuts and jobs act of 2018 cut the income tax of a corporation to a flat 21% for businesses classified as C corporations.

However, for C corporations that pay dividends to the shareholders, the shareholders end up paying tax on those dividends on their tax returns, and there is ultimately double taxation.

The dividends are classified as qualified or unqualified. The qualified dividend is if the individual has owned stock in the corporation for longer than 60 days. Qualified dividends have favorable tax rates and are taxed as long-term capital gain rates. The unqualified dividends are known as ordinary dividends and are taxed at the shareholders' personal tax rate.

Business formations that are considered pass-through entities are businesses where the profits are taxed at the owners' personal tax rate. So which types of business are pass-through entities?

Let us start with sole proprietorship and limited liability corporations. The sole proprietorship is a business where you are the owner and have the responsibility for the business finance while ensuring that the personal and business finances are separate.

Co-mingling personal and business funds can create tax problems if audited by the federal or state tax agency.

Similarly, limited liability corporations are also pass-through entities when the profit or loss is passed through to the owners' personal tax return without double taxation. Members of the limited liability corporation are required to pay self-employment tax. Both a sole proprietor and limited liability corporation will file the business income and expenses on their personal federal tax return under Schedule C.

Partnership returns are filed using form 1065. Partnerships are a bit more complicated, depending on the type of partnership.

A partnership is a business that is owned by two or more individuals. In a limited partnership, only one partner has unlimited liability, which means that the other partner(s) have limited control.

The general partner is responsible for the business debts should the business fail. While the limited partner has less control of the company, a limited liability partnership protects them from business debts and obligations if the business fails.

S Corporations are structured to avoid the double taxation of the C corporation. S corporations allow the profits and losses to pass through to the owners' tax return. The S corporation cannot have more than 100 shareholders. The tax return is filed on Form 1120S, and each shareholder will receive a K1 form, which reflects the profit or loss based on their percent of shares within the corporation. Other restrictions are that all shareholders of an S corporation must be US citizens.

A limited liability corporation can request to be taxed as an S corporation by filing forms with the Internal Revenue Service after registering with the Secretary of State.

Not only can you avoid double taxation, but registering as an S corporation also separates your business tax return from your personal return, which is better when applying for funding.

As an entrepreneur you can have a great plan in place,

understand your customer, hire the right employees, set realistic goals, build a wonderful brand, and have your finances in order, but if you cannot lead your staff, the business will suffer. The next section will cover leadership skills to lead your business to growth.

CHAPTER NINE

Become a Leader

Throughout my journey, one thing that I often observed is that many entrepreneurs lacked leadership skills. Upon the completion of my research for my doctoral dissertation at the University of Phoenix, I studied how the relationship of leadership influences the success or failure of female-owned businesses. I realized that a large part of why small businesses fail is due to the lack of leadership skills on how to lead the organization to future growth.

Leadership encompasses several styles. John C. Maxwell, a large influence in the leadership arena, explained leadership as the law of influence. The more influence, the greater the ability to lead increases. The five levels of leadership are known as the transformational leadership model because the leadership will adapt to the situation. The transformational leader focuses on the organization and behaviors that build follower commitment toward organizational objectives.

Leadership readiness is constant because the leadership skills will change with the situation. Aristotle stated, "*He who cannot be a good follower cannot be a good leader.*"

The leader-follower exchange theory, as introduced by Grean in 1970, emphasized the relationship between leader and subordinate. When leaders are trustworthy, followers will trust the leader. When the leader is honest, the follower will be authentic.

Committed leaders have motivated followers. Innovative leaders receive feedback from followers. Competent leaders have followers who are willing to learn. Courageous leaders have followers who are accepting. Leaders who take the initiative have followers who follow the vision.

As an entrepreneur and leader of your business, you will encounter individuals with various personalities. In most cases, the method to approach individuals with different personalities requires different communication approaches. One cannot approach someone social, fun-loving, and spontaneous with a direct, data-driven communications approach. Equally, one cannot approach someone who is no-nonsense with a less direct approach.

Entrepreneurs and leaders must exhibit high integrity, excellent communication skills, the ability to inspire and motivate others, hold others accountable, set clear goals, and have conflict resolution skills. According to Maxwell, developing a strategy for leadership should include position, permission, production, people development, and pinnacle.

If you begin your plan with employee development, you will empower your employees to learn and grow within the organization, which will result in a change of position, permission, and production. Employees will no longer follow because they must; they will follow because they want to make a difference in the business. Maxwell stated that successful people discover what they are good at; successful leaders find out what other people are good at.

As entrepreneurs, it is essential to develop a culture where the employees follow because they respect leadership. Developing a culture can be done by implementing a leadership model that incorporates four areas 1) Creating Mission/Vision, 2) Deliver Excellence, 3) Develop Self and Others, and 4) Lead Organizational Change.

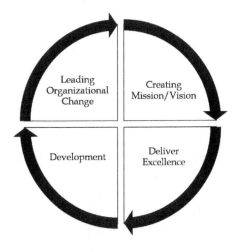

Creating vision and mission is centered on the organizational purpose for its customers and employees, including communicating effectively, establishing presentation skills, and strategic thinking. A leader without purpose would find it difficult to lead or gain followers.

Delivering excellence would necessitate the ability to make critical decisions, delegate tasks to the employees, focus on results, lead with integrity, and problem-solve.

Step three, leadership development and the

development of others, entails coaching, mentoring, listening, team building, developing time management, and creating value in others.

Finally, leading organizational change requires an understanding of when it is necessary to make management changes, allowing for innovation, inspiring and motivating others, and establishing organizational savvy.

Although each step of the model is essential to the leaders' success, step three carries the most weight. The development of self and others allows the leader, employees, and organization to grow, understand their market share, and become competitive.

Without excellent human capital, the organization cannot and will not grow. Additionally, experience in leading others is the best method for developing leaders. Coaching provides individualized feedback, and mentoring is informal support. Both are similar, although coaching tends to be formal and structured, where mentoring is relaxed and more personal. Developing employees and leadership for organizational sustainability is vital.

As an entrepreneur, it is essential to have a great vision. Understand that one alone cannot make that vision a reality. It requires a team that understands the vision and has a passion for making a change in others' lives with a sense of urgency for the future. It requires a shared motto to live the life you make for yourself.

LEADERSHIP STYLES

As an entrepreneur and leader of your organization, it is essential to understand your leadership style. The seven most common leadership styles are transactional, transformational, servant, bureaucratic, charismatic, democratic, and laissez-faire.

Transactional Leadership

Transactional leadership focuses on how the leader interacts with its followers — on how the leader provides transactional rewards or punishes its followers. The transactional leadership style demands the followers to agree to obey their leader and provide clarification of roles and goals. Transactional leaders appeal to the self-interest and benefit of the follower as a method of motivation. The followers are rewarded or punished based on their performance. This leadership style is useful for ambitious individuals; it is less efficient for employees who are not motivated by rewards.

Transformational Leadership

Transformational leadership is a style of leadership that offers high integrity and the ability to motivate others with a mission to transform the organization. The transformational leader appeals to the moral values of the follower to raise their consciousness on ethical issues and mobilize their energy.

The transformational leadership style creates a vision for the organization and inspires the followers to achieve the goals and objectives. Transformational leaders produce constructive changes in the followers and motivate followers in a positive direction.

Servant Leadership

Servant leaders lead by example and meet the needs of the team; the servant leader has high integrity and can achieve power because of their values, ideals, and ethics.

Bureaucratic Leadership

Bureaucratic leadership is one that relies on rules and procedures. The bureaucratic leaders ensure that the followers are completing the task according to the guidelines and standards. Bureaucratic leaders often manage or micromanage the employees who perform routine tasks.

Charismatic Leadership

Charismatic leaders are like transformational leaders, where they can motivate and inspire others. However, the difference is in the intent. Charismatic leaders focus on themselves and ambition; they may also believe they can do no wrong. Additionally, charismatic leadership is often risky, as they often misuse their power and the vision remains unchanged.

Democratic Leadership

The democratic leader has a participative style; they often run projects like a democracy. They inspire a collaborative spirit in their employees by encouraging that everyone works together, having the employees become actively involved in the decision-making process by including employee input and contribution. The democratic leader is less likely to hand down orders but works collaboratively with the team to get things done.

Laissez Faire Leadership

Laissez-faire leaders deliver the necessary tools and resources, and then step back and let their employee make decisions, solve problems, and get their work accomplished without worrying about the leader overseeing their every move.

What's your leadership style and leadership personality?

During my studies for my MBA, I participated in a leadership personality assessment known as DISC.

According to the DISC personality assessment, there are four types of behaviors that determine your leadership style: dominant, influencing, conscientious, and steady.

Deciding which of the behaviors you have, one or many can help you determine which leadership style best suits you.

First, let us define the different types of behaviors. The dominant behavior is a direct individual. They are firm with others and focused on goals and bottom-line results. The strengths of an individual with a dominant behavior is that are they are doers. They are able to get things done, have high leadership ability, and are decisive. However, they tend to be inflexible, impatient, and lack active listening, which could result in them failing to enjoy the journey.

People with influencing behavior are direct and open. They can be animated and spirited, but are often viewed as manipulative and can display impulsive behaviors in inappropriate situations. The strengths of a person with the influencing behavior style are that they are enthusiastic, persuasive, and sociable. Their weaker points are impatience, short attention spans, and they are easily bored.

The third behavior is conscientious. The individual with this type of style is very analytical and concerned with processes. They are persistent, systematic problem solvers. Also known as someone who views themselves as a perfectionist, serious, and disciplined. The strengths of a person who has a conscientious behavioral style are accuracy, dependability, follow-through, and organization. As possible weaknesses, they are prone to procrastination as well as being conservative and overly cautious.

The last behavior is steady. Individuals who possess a steady behavior style are open and indirect. They are unassertive, warm, and reliable. They are often identified as a person who is conforming, soft-hearted, and submissive. They are slow to make a decision and often need to know how others feel about the situation before acting. Steady-style strengths are caring for and loving others. However, their weakness is they are passive, exceedingly vulnerable, and easily manipulate or bullied.

When looking at the various leadership styles, you

may have traits from one or many of the leadership personality behaviors. For example, someone in the dominant behavior may find themselves as transactional or bureaucratic leaders. Still, they may also have behaviors that fit the influencing style.

There is no one perfect leadership style or behavior; there are many mixtures of how leaders act. However, understanding your leadership style and behavior will enable you, as an entrepreneur, to understand and lead your employees better. The importance of understanding your employees is critical to the success of your business.

True Story: There was an entrepreneur that had several employees. However, he did not understand the various personalities of the people he had working for him. He thought he could treat them all the same.

When it came to discipline, he disciplined them all in the same manner. He could not understand how the discipline would make some employees more motivated and focused, while others were unable to complete the task for several weeks.

This entrepreneur believed that if the latter group of employees didn't care as much as he did and were not loyal to the company. His thought process was that he treated them like family, gave them free lunch every day, and allowed them to come in late.

One would think that, in this era, everyone knows that no two people are the same, but we often try to treat them all the same way. It does not work. Some employees are motivated by money; others are motivated by the acknowledgement that they did a good job. And still others just want to do their job and go home.

Entrepreneurs often expect the employees to care as much about the business as they themselves do. That is never the case. Employees can buy into your mission and vision and be on board with the direction the company is going, but they will never care as much or more than you should.

Understanding your leadership style and behaviors will better equip you for leading your organization to sustainable growth. Remember, it's your business and the ultimate goal is success, so learn to become a great leader. Lead by example and the others will follow. Which leads me to building and growing your business. You have done all the planning, now let's build and grow.

CHAPTER TEN
Build and Grow

Build and Grow is the most exciting step in your pathway to entrepreneurship. The excitement of launching your business and the anticipation of whether customers will purchase your product or service also makes it the most nerve-wracking time.

But don't worry. By now, you have identified who your client is and created a great brand. By marketing your brand on social media and your website, customers will find you. Remember to set clear and attainable goals. We all want to believe that when we open our doors, customers will flood in and purchase everything. I would love to say that it is true, but the reality is: it's not. It takes time and a lot of work to build a significant client base and to develop a relationship that keeps those customers coming back for your product or service.

We have covered the start of your journey, innovation, the road map, creation, branding, finance, human capital, taxes, and leadership.

Understanding that starting and growing a business is not easy, the success of your business depends primarily on the amount of effort you place on increasing profits and promoting the brand. Ideally, you have already clearly defined your customer; now it's time to understand what your customer wants. This can be done through research or surveys, reviews, and feedback. The truth will enable you to develop a product or service that suits your customer's needs and wants.

Once you have that customer, take the extra step to make them feel special and let them know they are valued. Make sure that your customers' questions and concerns are answered in a timely fashion. Social media is a great place to get customer feedback, good and bad. As I mentioned earlier, customers' bad experiences could cause them to post negative things on social media, which can destroy everything you have worked so hard to build.

Just the same, positive feedback and responses on social media can quickly expand your customer base. Without a doubt, social media can provide incredibly positive results for your business without costing a lot of money, reaching hundreds and even thousands of people at once.

Engaging with your customers on social media keeps you relevant and helps you better understand them and their needs. This can guide you to create products or services to meet those needs.

Remember that it is crucial not to get into a posting war with someone who may post a negative comment. Take the information and fix the problem, apologize, and ensure it won't happen again. Above all, keep your integrity intact. If you get into a posting war, it could cause other customers to have a negative view of your company. Keep everything on social media light and positive.

Next, since you have already identified your market and who your competition is, you may want to establish a loyalty or rewards program that will keep the customer coming back, as the competition could offer them a better price or a discounted rate. Encourage loyalty by offering rewards, discounts, and promotions that they are the first to learn about; this will help the customer know they are valued and appreciated.

Building your brand and business also requires putting yourself out there every opportunity you have. Networking events allow you to showcase your new business while you meet other business owners and potential customers — or even an investor.

Networking is crucial in extending your brand and connecting with others who can help you build your business.

In finding what works, reevaluating the various approaches is often necessary. If you find that a tactic is not giving you a return on your investment, then eliminate it and try something else. Do not continue to pour money into something that is not working. For example, choosing to pay for social media ads, only to find that those ads are not bringing in customers. You need to reevaluate and ask: is it the message in the ad or is it the platform? Depending on what you find, you can try a different direction. There is no magical formula for keeping customers loyal, except for exceptional products and customer service. Customers will shop where they feel valued and appreciated if the product or service meets the quality standard.

Great Product + Great Service = Loyal Customers.

ACKNOWLEDGEMENT

Most who know me know that I am a life-long learner and am always willing to share the knowledge. This book came about shortly after completing my doctoral dissertation and graduating with the Doctor of Management degree.

I was done, with no more classes. Most would be excited; I was anxious. I have not been out of school for the past eight years and was having withdrawals. I would log in to the school portal every day looking for something to do, but nothing. The message would pop-up and say, *"You are not currently enrolled in a class."* Oh, yeah! After about three weeks, I decided I needed another project and felt it was time to write this book.

It was time to share my journey and knowledge on the steps to starting a business with the correct information. Many others and I started businesses with bad or wrong information and experienced unnecessary struggles.

The purpose of Get It Done is to help entrepreneurs — new, current, and future — to understand the journey of entrepreneurship and success.

AUTHOR'S BIO

Dr. Rose Lorenzo has over 30 years of entrepreneurial experience. Dr. Rose, as most call her, has owned and operated several companies and has more than 20 years in the banking and finance industry, with expertise in accounting, bookkeeping, tax preparation, corporate formations, leadership, management, and organizational development.

Dr. Rose has an undergraduate degree in Paralegal Studies and Criminal Justice Administration-Management, a Master's in Business Administration (MBA), and a Doctor of Management in Organizational Leadership degree from the University of Phoenix.

Dr. Rose is passionate about helping business owners learn to grow and sustain their businesses by providing them the business information to help them get started correctly, or to correct mistakes already made.

Dr. Rose is Co-Founder and Chief Executive Officer of Hackathon Jr., a non-profit organization that provides children with access to STEM education and preparing the next generation of leaders to solve problems with technology.

As a life-long learner, Dr. Rose is always willing to share the knowledge. This book came about shortly after completing her doctoral dissertation and graduating with the Doctor of Management degree. Dr. Rose wanted to share her journey and knowledge on the steps to starting a business with the correct information.

Many entrepreneurs start businesses with bad or wrong information and experience unnecessary struggles, thus contributing to the high rate of small business failures in the United States. Helping entrepreneurs with the development of a plan and the steps to get started could increase the rate of successful entrepreneurs in the United States and globally.

Can You Help?

Thank You for Reading My Book!

I really appreciate all your feedback, and I love hearing what you have to say.

I need your input to make the next version of this book and my future books better.

Please leave me an honest review on Amazon letting me know what you thought of the book.

Thanks so much!

Dr. Rose Emily Lorenzo